ALL SHALL BE WELL

A Spiritual Journal

FOR HOPE & ENCOURAGEMENT

HILDA ST. CLAIR

PARACLETE PRESS
BREWSTER, MASSACHUSETTS

2017 Second and Third printing
2016 First printing

All Shall Be Well: A Spiritual Journal for Hope and Encouragement

Copyright © 2016 by The Community of Jesus, Inc.

ISBN 978-1-61261-833-3

The Paraclete Press name and logo (dove on cross) are trademarks of Paraclete Press, Inc.

10 9 8 7 6 5 4 3

Published by Paraclete Press
Brewster, Massachusetts
www.paracletepress.com

Printed in the United States of America

Introduction

This journal has been for us a time of new beginnings. May you too receive something special from these pages: whether it's a new beginning, comfort, joy, insight, or a time to reconnect with other people and with God.

We wish you hope and encouragement on your particular journey, and may good things be waiting for you just around the next bend!

"All shall be well."

TERESA OF AVILA

LET NOTHING
DISTURB YOU.

LET NOTHING
FRIGHTEN YOU.

GOD ALONE
IS ENOUGH.

Write your fears in each of these boxes.

NOW MARK AN X OVER EACH ONE AND
WRITE UNDERNEATH EACH ONE,

"GOD IS BIGGER THAN THIS."

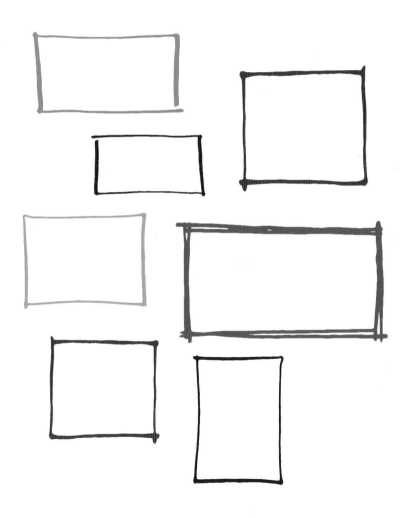

Our faith is a light.

JULIAN OF NORWICH

What lights up your life and heart?

WHAT WOULD YOU DO, WHO WOULD YOU HELP IF THE *sky's the limit?*

WRITE ABOUT IT HERE.

Allow your soul the freedom to

SING
DANCE
PRAISE
and
LOVE

TERESA OF AVILA

IMAGINE THAT YOUR SOUL
IS SINGING A ⁓ song.

Write the lyrics of that song.

GOD HAS ARRANGED EVERYTHING IN THE UNIVERSE.

HILDEGARD OF BINGEN

CIRCLE THE TOPICS IN WHICH YOU WOULD LIKE *God's help* TODAY:

Work

Friends

Health

Family

Finances

UNDERNEATH EACH ONE, WRITE HOW YOU WOULD LIKE EACH AREA TO LOOK IN YOUR LIFE.

Let gratitude for the past
inspire us with
trust for the future.

FRANÇOIS FÉNELON

LIST 5 PAST THINGS YOU ARE TRULY GRATEFUL FOR.

LIST 5 THINGS IN THE FUTURE YOU ARE ANXIOUS ABOUT.

BELOW THESE LISTS, WRITE ANY CONNECTIONS YOU SEE BETWEEN THE LISTS.

Past   Future

1.

2.

3.

4.

5.

THOSE WHO LOVE,

fly, run

and

rejoice

THEY ARE
FREE AND
UNRESTRAINED.

THOMAS à KEMPIS

DRAW 3 CHAINS AND IMAGINE THEM LOCKED AROUND YOU. WHAT IS EACH CHAIN CALLED?

IF *love* IS A KEY, HOW CAN IT UNLOCK EACH OF THESE CHAINS?

Anyone WHO TRULY LOVES GOD TRAVELS SECURELY

TERESA OF AVILA

on your journey called TODAY.

LIST 5 THINGS you want to put in your carry-on.

GIVE SPECIFIC EXAMPLES OF THINGS YOU MIGHT WANT TO CARRY: FAITH, POSITIVITY, PICTURES OF LOVED ONES, FLOWERS, YOUR FAVORITE BOOK—OR WHATEVER MEANS MOST TO YOU.

1.

2.

3.

4.

5.

THE
FULLNESS
OF JOY
is to see
God
in
everything.

JULIAN OF NORWICH

WHAT'S one of the *best* THINGS GOD HAS ever DONE FOR YOU?

WHAT'S one of the most *challenging* THINGS HE HAS EVER ASKED YOU TO GO THROUGH?

DRAW A SYMBOL FOR EACH. THEN DRAW A CIRCLE THAT ENCLOSES THEM BOTH.

CATHERINE OF SIENA

Be who God meant you to be and you will set the world on fire.

WHAT are your GIFTS and TALENTS? WHAT IS your PERSONAL PASSION? WRITE THEM IN THE FLAMES. IF YOU REALLY PURSUED ONE OF THEM, WHO MIGHT CATCH A SPARK FROM YOU? WRITE ABOUT THAT HERE.

IT IS PLEASANT TO RIDE
WHEN WE ARE CARRIED
BY
the grace of God

THOMAS à KEMPIS

DRAW a wagon that looks like *you* carrying your burdens.

DRAW a wagon that looks like **God** carrying your burdens.

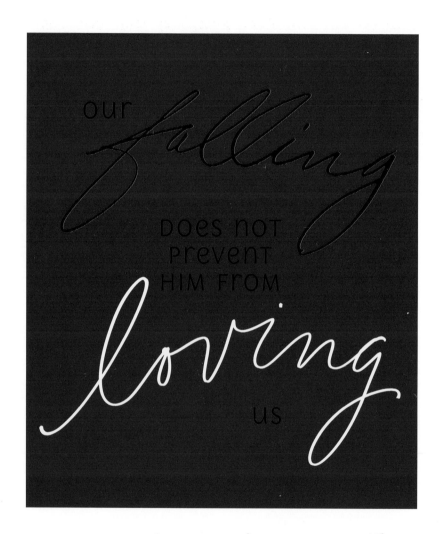

our *falling* does not prevent him from *loving* us

JULIAN OF NORWICH

There is an old saying THAT GOD CASTS OUR MISDEEDS INTO THE DEEPEST OCEAN WITH A SIGN THAT SAYS "NO FISHING!"

EVEN IF YOU HAVE EXPERIENCED FORGIVENESS FROM GOD AND PEOPLE, DO YOU EVER DRAW THINGS OUT AGAIN? WRITE HERE SOMETHING YOU WISH YOU HAD NEVER DONE. TELL GOD YOU'RE SORRY AND ACCEPT HIS FORGIVENESS. THEN USE A BLACK MARKER AND CROSS IT OUT FOREVER. AND REMEMBER,

NO FISHING!

So Sing! The song of rejoicing softens hearts

HILDEGARD OF BINGEN

Write THE WORDS TO YOUR FAVORITE song.

SING IT!

Circle your favorite words.

think
often

ABOUT
THE LOVING
KINDNESS
OF GOD.

THOMAS À KEMPIS

LIST 5 places in your life that tell you **God loves you.**

THINK about these places for one minute each. REPEAT OFTEN.

You pay God a compliment by asking great things of him

TERESA OF AVILA

Go ahead – ask him for something great. (you might make his day!) finish this letter:

"Dear God, I want to ask you for..."

And all shall be well.

JULIAN OF NORWICH

IN THE SPACES BELOW, WRITE WHAT IS
NOT WELL. THEN FOR EACH ONE, AFFIRM
BEING OPEN TO GOD'S GUIDANCE.

WRITE AT THE BOTTOM OF YOUR LIST,
"I give all this to you, God."

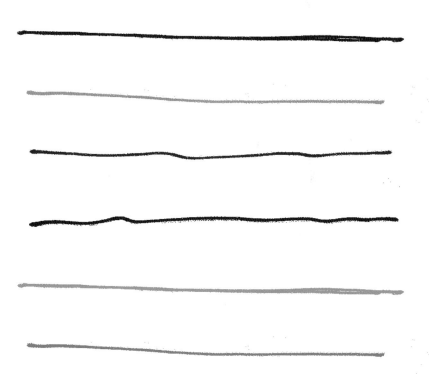

wisdom

IT IS
GREAT
WISDOM
TO KNOW
HOW
TO BE

SILENT.

JOHN OF THE CROSS

SET A TIMER FOR 5 MINUTES.

BE SILENT
AND STILL.

WHEN THE TIMER RINGS,
THANK GOD FOR THIS TIME.

REPEAT OFTEN.

THOMAS à KEMPIS

WHEN GOD IS

present

ALL IS WELL
AND
NOTHING
SEEMS

DIFFICULT.

DRAW 3 DIFFERENT SHAPES.
WRITE a DIFFICULTY IN YOUR LIFE IN EACH ONE.
NOW DRAW a SYMBOL FOR GOD IN THE MIDST OF
EACH ONE. *What difference does God's presence make?*

GOD IS
ON THE
journey
TOO.

TERESA OF AVILA

Draw your picture
IN THE BOX BELOW

List all the places –near and far–
TO WHICH YOU WANT TO TRAVEL WITH GOD

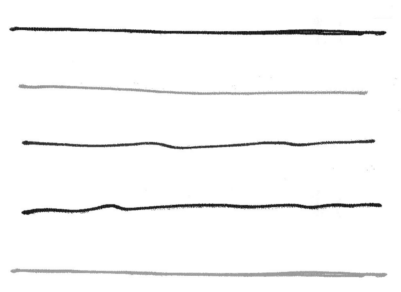

Wait for God's ordering

AND YOU WILL FIND
IT IS FOR YOUR
GOOD.

THOMAS à KEMPIS

WRITE DOWN A CIRCUMSTANCE WHEN
GOD WORKED THINGS OUT FOR YOUR
good.

How can recalling that help you to "wait" now?

TIME SPENT IN PRAYER IS NEVER WASTED

FRANÇOIS FÉNELON

For 3 days,

COMPARE THE TIME YOU SPEND ON SOCIAL MEDIA
OR TELEVISION AND THE TIME SPENT IN PRAYER.

HOW WOULD YOUR

LIFE

change

IF YOU REVERSED THAT TIME?

RUN TO *the Lord* AND BE COMFORTED.

JULIAN OF NORWICH

Tell God what's wrong.

TELL WHAT YOU NEED BY CIRCLING ANY OF
THE WORDS THAT APPLY (AND IF YOU WISH, FILL IN
THE BLANKS WITH YOUR OWN WORDS):

healing.

forgiveness.

a miracle.

peace.

a change of heart.

a friend who will listen.

a new perspective.

financial help.

_____,

_____.

we're rewarded not according to our work, but according to the measure of our love.

CATHERINE OF SIENA

In the first cup, DRAW IN THE WATER TO THE LEVEL OF HOW MUCH LOVE YOU HAVE SHOWN TO OTHERS IN THE PAST WEEK (A LITTLE? A LOT?).

In the second cup, DRAW IN THE WATER TO THE LEVEL OF HOW MUCH LOVE YOU HAVE RECEIVED IN THE PAST WEEK (A LITTLE? A LOT?).

Is there a correlation?

Now DRAW IN THE WATER LEVEL IN BOTH CUPS OF HOW MUCH LOVE YOU'D LIKE TO GIVE, AND TO RECEIVE.

This IS OUR LORD'S WILL: THAT OUR PRAYER AND OUR TRUST BE BOTH EQUALLY GREAT.

JULIAN OF NORWICH

write 3 brief prayers

in column 1 put what you are *asking* for.
in column 2 put what you are *trusting* for.

"GOD, I ASK
you FOR:"

"THEREFORE, GOD, I
TRUST you FOR:"

FOR UNTIL THE CORD
IS BROKEN,
THE BIRD CANNOT FLY.

JOHN OF THE CROSS

WHAT'S HOLDING YOU BACK?

In what area are you searching for more *freedom?*

If you were to break free...
write 3 words to describe the feeling, all
ending in ING.

_____ING

_____ING

_____ING

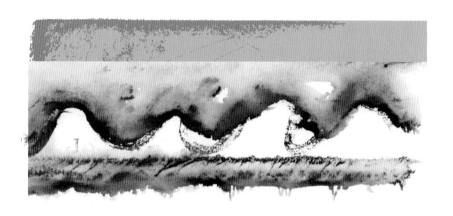

Above all, live in the present moment and God will give you all the grace you need.

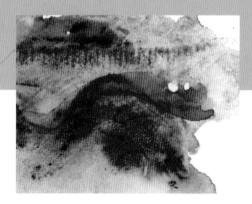

FRANÇOIS FÉNELON

close your eyes.

WHAT DO YOU HEAR?

WHAT DO YOU SMELL?

WHAT DO YOU FEEL?

WHAT DO YOU TASTE IN THIS MOMENT?

BREATHE DEEPLY

AND QUIETLY—AND THINK OF

energy

MOVING FROM YOUR

HEAD DOWN TO YOUR

TOES.

START BEING
BRAVE
ABOUT
every thing

CATHERINE OF SIENA

CHOOSING TO ACT IN THE MIDST OF FEAR

IS ONE ATTRIBUTE OF COURAGE. IN EACH OF THE 4 SECTIONS OF THIS SHIELD, WRITE ONE AREA IN WHICH YOU'D LIKE TO BE MORE COURAGEOUS. CHOOSE A PERSONAL MOTTO AND WRITE IT ON THE SCROLL. (SOME SAMPLES TO CHOOSE FROM ARE...STAND FIRM... GO FORWARD, PILGRIM...ALWAYS FAITHFUL...LIVE LIFE TO THE FULLEST... OR WRITE YOUR OWN.

IN TRIBULATION,
IMMEDIATELY
DRAW NEAR TO
GOD WITH
CONFIDENCE

JOHN ℃ THE CROSS

Write a prayer IN THE SPACE BELOW.

GOD, I LOVE YOU AND TRUST YOU.

God says,

REMAIN WITH ME
AND YOU WILL
FIND PEACE.

THOMAS à KEMPIS

Draw a circle and write GOD in it.

outside the circle draw 3 smaller circles; in each one write something you are afraid of.

Draw another circle putting these 3 things in the circle with GOD.

What difference does it make?

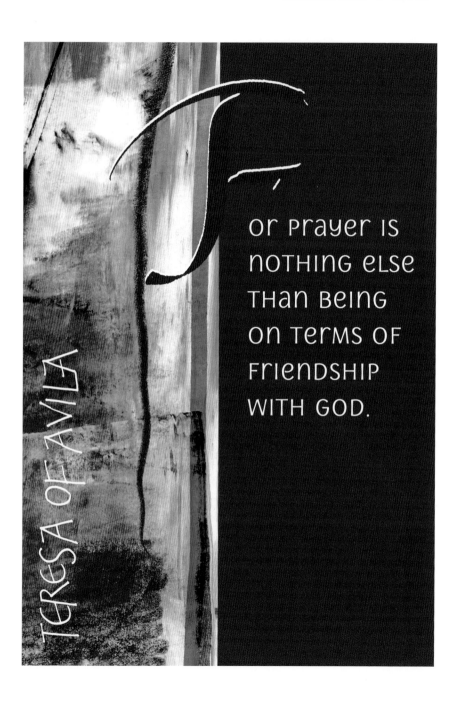

For prayer is nothing else than being on terms of friendship with God.

TERESA OF AVILA

What if
GOD CALLED YOU ON THE PHONE?

WHAT WOULD
YOU ASK HIM?

WHAT MIGHT
HE TELL YOU?

THE MYSTERY OF GOD
HUGS YOU IN ITS ALL~
ENCOMPASSING ARMS.

HILDEGARD OF BINGEN

WHAT COLORS REMIND YOU OF GOD?

COLOR IN THE WORD "GOD" BELOW WITH THOSE COLORS. ADD ANY DECORATIONS AROUND THE WORD THAT BRING YOU *joy.*

GOD

LIFE · LOVE · LIGHT
IN LIFE,
FAMILIARITY
IN LOVE,
GENTLE COURTESY
& IN LIGHT,
ENDLESS KINDNESS

JULIAN OF NORWICH

FAMILIAR, COURTEOUS, AND KIND

GOD IS THE BEST FRIEND ANYONE COULD ASK FOR.

See if you can thank him in 140 characters or less!

we **DO** MUCH WHEN WE **LOVE** MUCH.

THOMAS à KEMPIS

Write 3 things YOU WANT TO ACCOMPLISH TODAY.

1.

2.

3.

HOW WILL LOVE HELP YOU TO ACCOMPLISH EACH ONE?

ABIDE IN PEACE.

BANISH CARES.

Take no account of all that happens.

JOHN ⚬f the CROSS

List your cares.

THEN, ONE AT A TIME, CROSS THEM OUT AND WRITE

PEACE

It is
love alone
that gives
worth
to all
things.

TERESA OF AVILA

Who and what do I love?

WRITE THEM IN THESE FIRST 4 HEARTS, AND GIVE THANKS FOR THEM AS YOU DO.

Who and what do you feel you need to give more love to?

WRITE THEM IN THE SECOND 4 HEARTS, AND GIVE THANKS FOR THEM AS YOU DO.

To a brave man, good and bad luck are like his left and right hand. He uses both.

CATHERINE OF SIENA

FILL IN THE BLANKS. DOES YOUR PERCEPTION OF WHETHER SOMETHING IS "GOOD" OR "BAD" LUCK CHANGE ACCORDING TO HOW YOU PERCEIVE IT?

GOOD LUCK experiences

BAD LUCK experiences

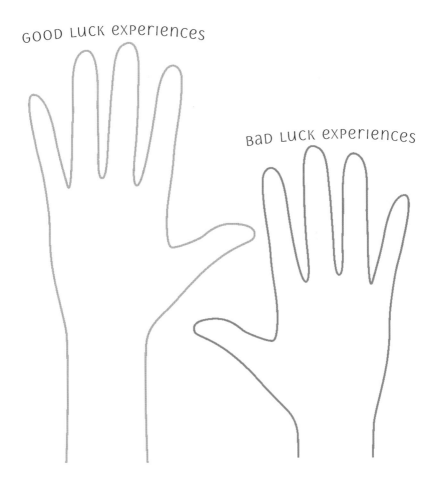

In the darkest moments, bright flows the river of God.

JOHN of the CROSS

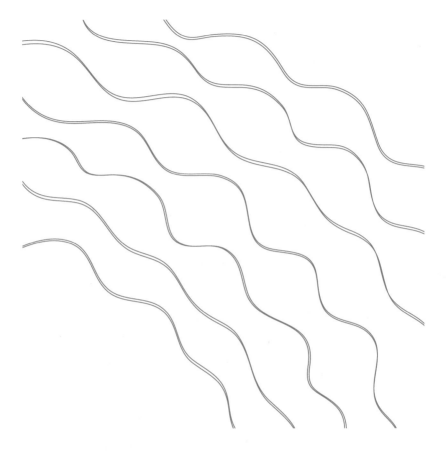

Write down a DIFFICULT EXPERIENCE
YOU ONCE HAD. CALL TO MIND ANY GLINTS OF
LIGHT YOU FOUND IN THE MIDST OF IT. WRITE
THEM IN THE RIVER.

HILDEGARD OF BINGEN

GOD'S GRACE
ALSO REWARDS
THOSE WHO
BEND AND FALL.

LIST THE TIMES WHEN YOUR FAILURES OR MISTAKES HAD A *good outcome*.

We need
no wings to go
in search of Him

TERESA OF AVILA

Lie Down, Breathe Deeply,

AND THINK ABOUT GOD'S PRESENCE
WITHIN YOU.

NOW, IN THE SPACE BELOW WRITE
HOW THAT MADE YOU FEEL.

God withholds
himself

from no one
who perseveres.

TERESA OF AVILA

Fill in the two columns below:

"TOUGH STUFF
IN MY LIFE"

"WHAT IS GOD SAYING
TO ME ABOUT THIS TODAY?"

The human heart is always drawn by love.

CATHERINE OF SIENA

Name 5 people WHO HAVE BEEN THERE FOR YOU WHEN YOU WERE STRUGGLING THE MOST. WRITE THEIR NAMES BELOW, AND AFTER EACH NAME WRITE *"Thank you"* (AND THEN CONSIDER THANKING THEM IN PERSON).

1.

2.

3.

4.

5.

Love

WHERE
THERE IS
NO LOVE,
PUT LOVE
AND YOU
WILL FIND
LOVE.

JOHN OF THE CROSS

DIFFICULT SITUATIONS

HOW I COULD ADD LOVE TO THEM

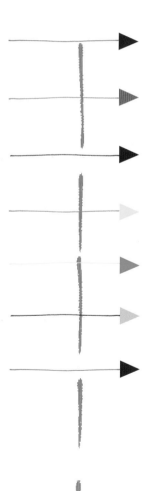

We do not know the strength of our own hearts, nor the power of God.

FRANÇOIS FÉNELON

WHAT'S THE GREATEST CHALLENGE IN YOUR LIFE RIGHT NOW?

Write it here AND THEN WRITE 3 TIMES

"I CAN DO THIS. GOD WILL HELP ME."

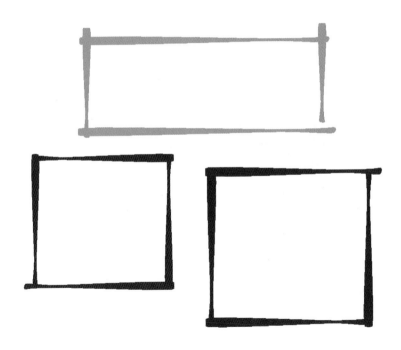

IF A MAN WISHES TO BE
SURE OF THE ROAD HE
TREADS ON, HE MUST
CLOSE HIS EYES AND
WALK IN THE DARK.

JOHN OF THE CROSS

Copy 3 times ON THE ROAD BELOW:

"GO IN PEACE. THE WAY IN WHICH YOU GO IS UNDER THE EYE OF THE LORD." THEN ASK GOD FOR A GIFT OF CONFIDENCE FOR TODAY.

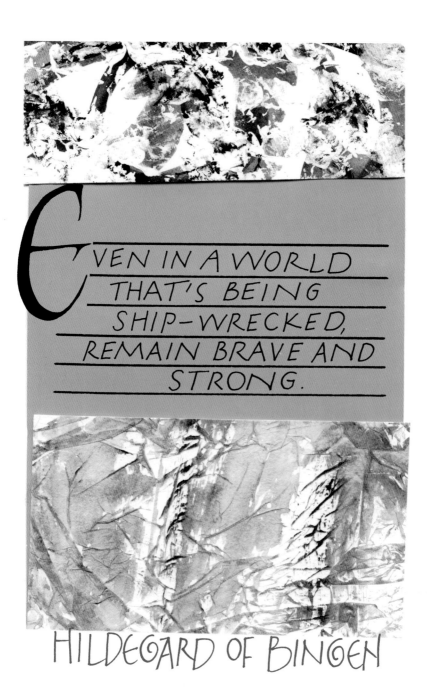

EVEN IN A WORLD THAT'S BEING SHIP-WRECKED, REMAIN BRAVE AND STRONG.

HILDEGARD OF BINGEN

NAME FIVE PEOPLE
(living or from history)
WHOM YOU'D LIKE TO HAVE WITH YOU IN A SHIPWRECK. WHAT QUALITY DOES EACH ONE OF THEM HAVE THAT YOU ADMIRE?

1.

2.

3.

4.

5.

Love Does not stay idle.

Catherine of Siena

WHERE AM I STANDING STILL?

WHERE AM I MOVING?

Circle THE ITEM IN EACH COLUMN THAT SEEMS MOST IMPORTANT TO THINK MORE ABOUT.

MOST PEOPLE
I ASK LITTLE
FROM. I TRY
TO GIVE THEM
MUCH, AND
EXPECT NOTHING
IN RETURN AND
I DO VERY WELL
IN THE BARGAIN.

FRANÇOIS FÉNELON

LIST 5 important relationships you have. Make a note of what you can give to each today.

HILDEGARD OF BINGEN

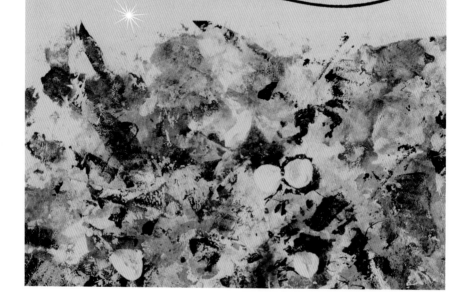

LOVE EXCELS
FROM THE DEPTHS
TO BEYOND
THE STARS.

THINK ABOUT THE
VASTNESS OF GOD'S LOVE FOR YOU.

Think of people WHOM YOU WOULD LIKE TO EXPERIENCE GOD'S LOVE TODAY—WRITE THEIR NAMES IN THE STARS.

CATHERINE OF SIENA

You are all
trees of love.

Draw your life

as a tree WITH WITH 6 rOOTS & 6 BLOSSOMS.

In the blossoms WRITE IN THE 6 THINGS
you wanT TO HaVE BLOSSOMING IN your LIFE.

In the roots WRITE 6 THINGS THAT WILL
neeD TO "FeeD" THE Tree TO HeLP PrODUCE THESE
BLOSSOMS.

In the evening of life, we will be judged on love alone.

JOHN of the CROSS

Make a list BELOW OF ALL
THE PEOPLE YOU LOVE, AND
WHAT YOU LOVE ABOUT THEM.

DRAW HEARTS AROUND THE PAGE.
ADD MORE HEARTS TO SYMBOLIZE MORE LOVE.

IF YOU CONSIDER
the dignity of the Giver

NO GIFT WILL SEEM
TOO LITTLE TO VALUE.

THOMAS à KEMPIS

LIST THREE LITTLE "GIFTS" IN YOUR LIFE THAT
YOU TAKE FOR GRANTED

*Take time to thank God
for each one.*

DO THEY SEEM ANY BIGGER TO YOU NOW?

1.

2.

3.

gained

FREQUENTLY A BIG ADVANTAGE CAN
BE GAINED BY KNOWING HOW TO
GIVE IN AT THE RIGHT MOMENT.

FRANÇOIS FÉNELON

1   2   3   4   5   6   7   8   9   10

Are you OPINIONATED or somewHat
of a *pushover*? GIVING In can
seem LIKe a weakness.

Can you recall a TIMe WHen you DeFerreD To
someone eLse's IDea? WriTe any aDVantages you
noTIceD THaT came OF THIS experience.

wind of God

THE WIND
OF GOD IS
always BLOWING...
BUT YOU MUST
HOIST your sail.

FRANÇOIS FÉNELON

IF YOU WERE A SHIP, —what would your name be?

WHERE WOULD YOU LIKE TO GO WITH GOD?

Below, draw a ship—

WITH FULL SAILS UNFURLED.

AND MAKE A SIGN POINTING TO WHERE IT IS GOING.

GO OUTDOORS OR GO TO AN OPEN WINDOW.
BREATHE THE FRESH AIR,
AND TALK TO GOD ABOUT SOMETHING EITHER LARGE
OR SMALL, BUT IMPORTANT TO YOU.

⤳ *What do you hear?*

⤳ *What do you feel?*

DENY YOUR DESIRES
AND YOU WILL
FIND WHAT YOUR
HEART
LONGS FOR.

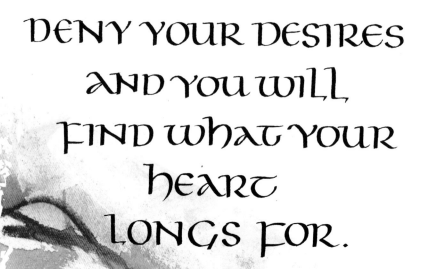

JOHN OF THE CROSS

LIST BELOW WHAT YOUR MIND DESIRES. ON THE OTHER SIDE, LIST WHAT YOUR HEART LONGS FOR.

How different are the two lists?

HEAD   HEART

Thus am I—a feather on the breath of God

HILDEGARD OF BINGEN

IMAGINE THAT YOU ARE A
feather.
WRITE ABOUT A TIME WHEN LIFE BLEW
YOU SOMEWHERE UNEXPECTED.

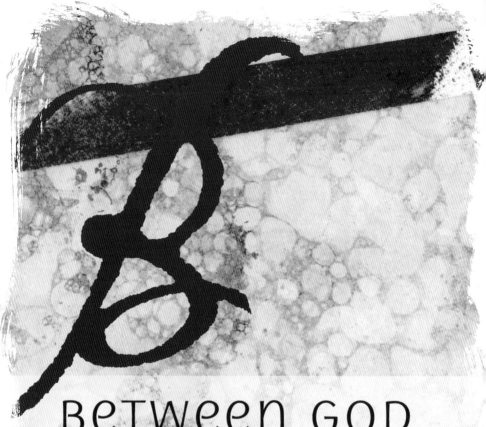

BETWEEN GOD
AND THE SOUL
THERE IS NO BETWEEN.

JULIAN OF NORWICH

Name a time or place THAT GOD TOUCHED YOUR HEART IN A *surprising way.*

THERE IS THE MUSIC
OF HEAVEN
IN ALL THINGS

HILDEGARD OF BINGEN

Imagine yourself relaxing in heaven with friends.

WHAT MUSIC WOULD YOU HOPE TO HEAR HEAVEN'S CHOIR OR ORCHESTRA PLAYING?

LIST THE TITLES HERE OF FIVE SONGS YOU KNOW OR OF SONGS YOU MAKE UP.

1.

2.

3.

4.

5.

Proclaim the truth and do not be silent through fear.

CATHERINE OF SIENA

LIST 5 THINGS you know are true.
CIRCLE THE ONE you plan to speak up about today.

1.

2.

3.

4.

5.

The more you say,
the less people remember.

FRANÇOIS FÉNELON

WRITE 3 **heartfelt** THINGS YOU'D
LIKE TO SAY TO GOD TODAY
(EACH ONE IN 3 WORDS OR LESS.)

1.

2.

3.

Offer happy praises in simplicity and love.

HILDEGARD OF BINGEN

write — *your own*
song of praise
USING WORDS LIKE THESE:

PRAISE GOD IN THE HEAVENS.

PRAISE HIM FOR HIS GREATNESS.

PRAISE HIM WITH HARPS AND DANCING.

LET ALL PEOPLE EVERYWHERE PRAISE GOD!

FOR FURTHER READING

Carmen Acevedo Butcher. *St. Hildegard of Bingen: A Spiritual Reader*. Brewster, MA: Paraclete Press, 2013.

Catherine of Siena. *Little Talks with God*. Paraclete Press, 2010.

François Fénelon. *The Complete Fénelon*. Robert J. Edmonson, CJ, editor. Paraclete Press, 2008.

John of the Cross. *Ascent of Mount Carmel*. Paraclete Press, 2010.

Fr. John-Julian, OJN. *The Complete Julian of Norwich*. Paraclete Press, 2009.

Fr. John-Julian, OJN. *The Complete* Imitation of Christ. Paraclete Press, 2012.

Julian of Norwich. *Revelations of Divine Love*, Deluxe Edition. Fr. John-Julian, OJN, editor. Paraclete Press. 2013.

Thomas à Kempis. *The Imitation of Christ*. Hal M. Helms, editor. Paraclete Press, 2008.

Teresa of Avila. *A Little Daily Wisdom: Through the Year with Saint Teresa of Avila*. Bernard Bangley, editor. Paraclete Press, 2011.

ABOUT PARACLETE PRESS

WHO WE ARE

Paraclete Press is a publisher of books, recordings, and DVDs on Christian spirituality. Our publishing represents a full expression of Christian belief and practice—from Catholic to Evangelical, from Protestant to Orthodox.

We are the publishing arm of the Community of Jesus, an ecumenical monastic community in the Benedictine tradition. As such, we are uniquely positioned in the marketplace without connection to a large corporation and with informal relationships to many branches and denominations of faith.

WHAT WE ARE DOING

PARACLETE PRESS BOOKS | Paraclete publishes books that show the richness and depth of what it means to be Christian. Although Benedictine spirituality is at the heart of who we are and all that we do, we publish books that reflect the Christian experience across many cultures, time periods, and houses of worship. We publish books that nourish the vibrant life of the church and its people.

We have several different series, including the bestselling Paraclete Essentials and Paraclete Giants series of classic texts in contemporary English; Voices from the Monastery—men and women monastics writing about living a spiritual life today; our award-winning Paraclete Poetry series as well as the Mount Tabor Books on the arts; bestselling gift books for children on the occasions of baptism and first communion; and the Active Prayer Series that brings creativity and liveliness to any life of prayer.

MOUNT TABOR BOOKS | Paraclete's newest series, Mount Tabor Books, focuses on the arts and literature as well as liturgical worship and spirituality, and was created in conjunction with the Mount Tabor Ecumenical Centre for Art and Spirituality in Barga, Italy.

PARACLETE RECORDINGS | From Gregorian chant to contemporary American choral works, our recordings celebrate the best of sacred choral music composed through the centuries that create a space for heaven and earth to intersect. Paraclete Recordings is the record label representing the internationally acclaimed choir Gloriæ Dei Cantores, praised for their "rapt and fathomless spiritual intensity" by *American Record Guide*; the Gloriæ Dei Cantores Schola, specializing in the study and performance of Gregorian chant; and the other instrumental artists of the Arts Empowering Life Foundation.

Paraclete Press is also privileged to be the exclusive North American distributor of the recordings of the Monastic Choir of St. Peter's Abbey in Solesmes, France, long considered to be a leading authority on Gregorian chant.

PARACLETE VIDEO | Our DVDs offer spiritual help, healing, and biblical guidance for a broad range of life issues including grief and loss, marriage, forgiveness, facing death, bullying, addictions, Alzheimer's, and spiritual formation

Learn more about us at our website:
www.paracletepress.com or phone us
toll-free at 1.800.451.5006

SCAN
TO
READ
MORE

Love Never Fails

A Journal to be Inspired by the Power of Love
HILDA ST. CLAIR
ISBN 978-1-61261-832-6 | $15.99 | Paperback

> *"Love is patient, love is kind. It does not envy,*
> *it does not boast, it is not proud."*
> *1 Corinthians 13:4 (NIV)*

Carefully chosen quotes from Mahatma Gandhi, Wendell Berry, Mother Teresa, Paul Coelho, and many others are hand-lettered and paired with joyful paintings and interactive exercises that will help the reader to explore the idea of a love which "hopes all things, bears all things and believes all things" in their own life.

1 Corinthians 13 has become an almost universal text describing the attributes of love. This text forms the framework for each section of the book. Each entry includes an inspired quote, uplifting artwork and a writing prompt that will lead the reader to new paths of reflection, revelation, and creativity.

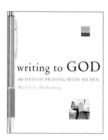

Writing to God

40 Days of Praying with My Pen
RACHEL HACKENBERG
ISBN 978-1-55725-879-3 | $15.99 | Paperback

"Praying by writing takes a prayer out of my head and makes praying a whole-body exercise: my creativity is sparked, my spirit fully focused, my muscles employed, my sense of touch and awareness of breath heightened. I felt more connected to prayer than I had ever experienced before."
—Rachel Hackenberg

Writing to God offers forty insightful days of prayer and personal reflection. With poems and thoughts to prompt your own prayers, *Writing to God* will inspire you when you feel dry, help you voice your deepest complaints and greatest joys, and surprise you with fresh perspectives on God.

Available from most booksellers or through Paraclete Press:
www.paracletepress.com | 1-800-451-5006